ALIEN
Conspiracy
THEORIES

by Ellis M. Reed

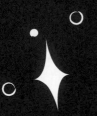

CAPSTONE PRESS
a capstone imprint

Bright Idea Books are published by Capstone Press
1710 Roe Crest Drive, North Mankato, Minnesota 56003
www.mycapstone.com

Library of Congress Cataloging-in-Publication Data
Names: Reed, Ellis M., 1992- author.
Title: Alien conspiracy theories / by Ellis M. Reed.
Description: North Mankato, Minnesota : Capstone Press, [2020] | Series:
   Aliens | Includes index. | Audience: Grade 4 to 6.
Identifiers: LCCN 2019003130 (print) | LCCN 2019005074 (ebook) | ISBN
   9781543571127 (ebook) | ISBN 9781543571042 (hardcover) | ISBN 9781543574913 (pbk.)
Subjects: LCSH: Unidentified flying objects--Sightings and encounters--United
   States--Juvenile literature. | Government information--United
   States--Juvenile literature. | Conspiracies--United States--Juvenile literature.
Classification: LCC TL789.4 (ebook) | LCC TL789.4 .R44 2020 (print) | DDC
   001.942--dc23
LC record available at https://lccn.loc.gov/2019003130

Editorial Credits
Editor: Claire Vanden Branden
Designer: Becky Daum
Production Specialist: Melissa Martin

Photo Credits
iStockphoto: Devrimb, 12–13, Pojbic, 15, Steve Debenport, 6–7; Newscom: Mirrorpix, 18; Rex Features: Chris Balcombe, 24; Shutterstock Images: Daemon Barzai, 23, Fer Gregory, 16–17, 26–27, footageclips, 20–21, ktsdesign, 30–31, Pavel Chagochkin, cover, Raggedstone, 5, tsuneomp, 11, 28, Ursatii, 8–9

Design Elements: Shutterstock Images, Red Line Editorial

Printed in the United States of America.
PA70

TABLE OF CONTENTS

CHAPTER 1

THE MEN in Black

It was a regular day in 1947. Harold Dahl went to Puget Sound in Washington. He was there with his son and their dog. They were collecting logs. They took a boat on the water.

Dahl looked at the sky. He saw something strange. Six shapes were flying over his boat. Suddenly one of the shapes fell. Pieces of it crashed to the ground. Dahl took photos.

The flying objects Harold Dahl saw were shaped like donuts.

In many movies, the MIB is an organization created by the government. It is top secret.

THE NEXT DAY

A strange man visited Dahl the next day. He wore a black suit. The man said he knew about the shapes. He told Dahl not to talk about them. Bad things would happen to Dahl if he did.

Other people have told stories about seeing Men in Black (MIB). Some stories said MIB wore sunglasses. Some had weird skin. MIB showed up after someone saw an **alien** or a **UFO**. They wanted the person to keep quiet about what they saw.

Dahl later said he made everything up.

Some people think it was a lie all along.

Others think he changed his story.

THEY KNEW TOO MUCH

Author Gray Barker wrote a book in 1956. It is called *They Knew Too Much About Flying Saucers*. It made many people believe in the MIB.

People still wonder if Dahl really saw a UFO.

CHAPTER 2

AREA 51

The MIB are an alien **conspiracy theory**. There are many different theories. One is that the U.S. government knows about aliens. Many people think it is hiding alien bodies.

Some people believe alien bodies are hidden inside Area 51.

Some people believe the government studies UFOs at Area 51.

HIDING UFOS

In 1947 a strange object crashed near Roswell, New Mexico. People think it was a UFO. They believe the government hid it at Area 51.

Area 51 is a military base in Nevada. Its work is top secret. There are signs telling people to stay away. People think this is because UFOs are hidden there. Others think the government is not hiding anything.

CHAPTER 3

CROP
Circles

Early one morning a farmer stepped outside. He looked at his cornfield. There was a huge **crop circle** in his field. He did not know how it was made. It was not there the day before.

Most crop circles
are made at night.
Then people discover
them the next day.

Many crop circles were made in England in the 1970s and 1980s. Some thought people could not have made them. They could not find footprints or tire tracks. People believed aliens made the circles.

Some people think aliens made crop circles using their spaceships.

Crop circles need to be made very carefully so that no footprints are seen.

Many years later people found out the truth. It was not aliens. It was two men named Doug Bower and Dave Chorley. The men made more than 200 crop circles. They made them with ropes and boards. This hid their footprints.

Crop circle shapes are made by flattening some corn stalks but not others.

Soon other people made crop circles. Many used Bower and Chorley's **method**. Most people today know people made the shapes. However, some people still believe some crop circles cannot be explained. They think aliens still make some of them.

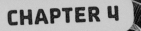

CHAPTER 4

WORLD
Leaders

Some people believe aliens have visited Earth. Others believe they live here. Some say **reptilians** are taking over the world.

These aliens look like lizards. Stories say they can change form. This makes them look like people. Other stories say they came to Earth long ago. They say world leaders are really these aliens.

Believers think reptilians came to Earth from other planets.

David Icke is famous for believing reptilians secretly control the world.

Some past U.S. presidents are said to be reptilians. Both George W. Bush and Bill Clinton are on the list. Barack Obama is said to be one too.

There are ways to tell if someone is a reptilian. Green or blue eyes are thought to be one sign. Another sign is loving science. But believers say anyone could be a reptilian.

DAVID ICKE

One believer is David Icke. He wrote *The Biggest Secret*. The book talks about reptilians' history on Earth.

Sometimes strange things happen on Earth. Some things cannot be explained. Many people come up with their own ideas. They think it always comes back to aliens.

People love to investigate alien conspiracy theories.

alien
a creature not from Earth

conspiracy theory
a belief that a person or group
is hiding something

crop circle
a large pattern in a field of
corn made of circles and
other shapes

method
a way of doing something

reptilian
a shapeshifting alien that
looks like a lizard

UFO
an unidentified flying object

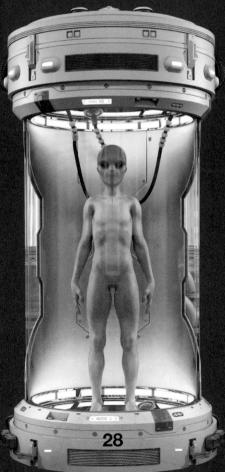

TRIVIA

1. The MIB have been featured in video games, movies, books, TV shows, and even theme park rides.

2. In the 1990s the U.S. government admitted that it had hidden information about Roswell. People thought this would prove that aliens existed. But instead the government was hiding Project Mogul. This was a top-secret experiment involving bombs.

FIND THE EVIDENCE

Many people believe in alien conspiracy theories. They say that they have evidence that aliens exist. But sometimes this evidence may seem fake. The person with the evidence could be making it up. Pick one of the conspiracies from this book. Then look for evidence about the conspiracy. Does the evidence seem real or fake? How might you tell? Write a paragraph about what you find.

FURTHER RESOURCES

Interested in learning more about conspiracy theories? Check out these resources:

CBC Kids: What Exactly Are UFOs?
https://www.cbc.ca/kidscbc2/the-feed/what-exactly-are-ufos

Krieger, Emily: *Real or Fake? Book 3.* Washington, D.C.: National Geographic Kids, 2018.

Reed, Ellis M. *Roswell.* Aliens. North Mankato, Minn.: Capstone Press, 2020.

Want to know about other alien topics? Take a look at these resources:

NASA Space Place: Voyagers to the Stars
https://spaceplace.nasa.gov/voyager-to-stars/en

National Geographic Kids: Alien Sea
https://kids.nationalgeographic.com/explore/space/alien-sea/#alien-sea-1.jpg

INDEX